PHYLLIS J. LE P

CARING
—FOR—
PHYSICAL
NEEDS

*8 Studies for Groups
or Individuals*
With Notes for Leaders

CARING PEOPLE BIBLE STUDIES

INTERVARSITY PRESS
DOWNERS GROVE, ILLINOIS, USA
LEICESTER, ENGLAND

InterVarsity Press, USA, is the book-publishing division of InterVarsity Christian Fellowship, a student movement active on campus at hundreds of universities, colleges and schools of nursing in the United States of America, and a member movement of the International Fellowship of Evangelical Students. For information about local and regional activities, write Public Relations Dept., InterVarsity Christian Fellowship, 6400 Schroeder Rd., P.O. Box 7895, Madison, WI 53707-7895.

Inter-Varsity Press, UK, is the book-publishing division of the Universities and Colleges Christian Fellowship (formerly the Inter-Varsity Fellowship), a student movement linking Christian Unions in universities and colleges throughout the United Kingdom and the Republic of Ireland, and a member movement of the International Fellowship of Evangelical Students. For information about local and national activities write to UCCF, 38 De Montfort Street, Leicester LE1 7GP.

Some of the studies in this guide are adapted from studies written by Nurses Christian Fellowship staff.

Cover photograph: Michael Goss

USA ISBN 0-8308-1196-6
UK ISBN 0-85111-335-4

Printed in the United States of America

15	14	13	12	11	10	9	8	7	6	5	4	3	2	1
03	02	01	00	99	98	97	96	95	94	93	92	91		

Getting the Most from Caring People Bible Studies

Caring People Bible Studies are designed to show how God equips us to help others who are in need. They reveal what the Bible has to say about the pain we will all face in life and what we can do to care for friends, family, neighbors and even strangers who experience pain.

The passages you will study will be thought-provoking, challenging, inspiring and practical. They will show you how to focus on others, but they will also help you focus on yourself. Why? Because these guides are not designed merely to convince you of the truthfulness of some idea. Rather, they are intended to allow biblical truths to renew your heart and mind.

These Bible studies are inductive rather than deductive. In other words, the author will lead us to discover what the Bible says about a particular topic through a series of questions rather than simply telling us what she believes. Therefore, the studies are thought-provoking. They help us to think about the meaning of the passage so that we can truly understand what the biblical writer intended to say.

Additionally, these studies are personal. At the end of each study, you'll be given an opportunity to make a commitment to respond. And you will find guidance for prayer as well. Finally, these studies are versatile. They are designed for student, professional, neighborhood and/or church groups. They are also effective for individual study.

How They're Put Together

Caring People Bible Studies have a distinctive format. Each study takes about forty-five minutes in a group setting or thirty minutes in personal study—unless you choose to take more time. The guides have a workbook format with space for writing responses to each question. This is ideal for personal study and allows group members to prepare in advance for the discussion. At the end of the guides are some notes for leaders. They describe how to lead a group discussion, give helpful tips on group dynamics, suggest ways to deal with problems which may arise during the discussion, and provide additional background information on certain questions. With such helps, someone with little or no experience can lead an effective study.

Suggestions for Individual Study

1. As you begin the study, pray that God will help you understand and apply the passages to your life. Pray that he will show you what kinds of action he would have you take as a result of your time of study.

2. In your first session take time to read the introduction to the entire study. This will orient you to the subject at hand and the author's goals for the studies.

3. Read the short introduction to the study.

4. Read and reread the suggested Bible passage to familiarize yourself with it.

5. A good modern translation of the Bible, rather than the King James Version or a paraphrase, will give you the most help. The New International Version, the New American Standard Bible and the Revised Standard Version are all recommended. However, the questions in this guide are based on the New International Version.

6. Use the space provided to respond to the questions. This will help you express your understanding of the passage clearly.

7. It might be good to have a Bible dictionary handy. Use it to look up any unfamiliar words, names or places.

8. Take time with the final question in each study to commit yourself to action and/or a change in attitude.

Suggestions for Group Study

1. Come to the study prepared. Follow the suggestions for individual study mentioned above. You will find that careful preparation will greatly enrich your time spent in group discussion.

2. Be willing to participate in the discussion. The leader of your group will not be lecturing. Instead, he or she will be encouraging the members of the group to discuss what they have learned. The leader will be asking the questions that are found in this guide.

3. Stick to the topic being discussed. Your answers should be based on the verses which are the focus of the discussion and not on outside authorities such as commentaries or speakers.

4. Be sensitive to the other members of the group. Listen attentively when they describe what they have learned. You may be surprised by their insights! When possible, link what you say to the comments of others. Also, be affirming whenever you can. This will encourage some of the more hesitant members of the group to participate.

5. Be careful not to dominate the discussion. We are sometimes so eager to express our thoughts that we leave too little opportunity for others to respond. By all means participate! But allow others to also.

6. Expect God to teach you through the passage being discussed and through the other members of the group. Pray that you will have an enjoyable and profitable time together, but also that as a result of the study, you will find ways that you can take action individually and/or as a group.

7. We recommend that groups follow a few basic guidelines, and that these guidelines be read at the beginning of the first session. The guidelines, which you may wish to adapt to your situation, are:

☐ Anything said in the group is considered confidential and will not be discussed outside the group unless specific permission is given to do so.

☐ We will provide time for each person present to talk if he or she feels comfortable doing so.

☐ We will talk about ourselves and our own situations, avoiding conversation about other people.

☐ We will listen attentively to each other.

☐ We will be very cautious about giving advice.

☐ We will pray for each other.

8. If you are the group leader, you will find additional suggestions at the back of the guide.

Introducing Caring for Physical Needs

I enjoy thinking about the people who have touched my family's lives by meeting our physical needs. Most of the times we were not in desperate situations. Yet people chose to communicate to us their love and God's love through making our lives easier and carrying some of our load.

For instance, our basement flooded when my husband, Andy, was sick and our fourth child was a newborn. People came, cleared out the boxes, swept out the water, and took home loads of soaked baby clothes that I had stored in boxes in a very *organized* fashion. They brought the clothes back clean and folded. Best of all I felt *organized* again.

Friends brought meals after the births of our children. We loved the great food. It was fun not knowing what was coming for supper and being surprised by it. But even better was the way it eased the whole adjustment of adding another little person to our home by having one less duty to perform.

I hate grocery shopping. With four growing children it is a huge monthly chore in the midst of all the other demands in my life. A friend has lightened that load tremendously. She gives of her own time and energy to help me with the shopping. There are times, when my energy is especially low, just knowing that she is going with me is the encouragement I need to get the job done.

When Philip was hospitalized with pneumonia as an infant, either Andy or I was at his bedside around the clock. Meanwhile, Stephen and Susan received great care from friends. In the midst of our concern for Philip, the burden was much lighter knowing the other two were in good hands.

Teams of people have helped us ease the pain of adding two rooms to our house. Some put up wallboard. Others papered those same walls. Some helped me clean, another helped stain wood. One person spent part of his holiday weekend helping Andy hook up the plumbing while his wife varnished wood-work. The chaos was calmed a bit, and the ordeal moved more quickly because of their help. This meeting of our physical needs came at the time that we were wondering if we would really make it through the project.

We have a friend who loves to garden and to make yards more beautiful. She has shared this gift with us. Our yard is lovely because of her time and effort. She offered her care for us in this way as a result of a passing comment I made about the difficulty we were having in keeping up with our yard. She picked up a cue that I did not even know that I had dropped.

Part of the joy of receiving from each of these people is the graciousness with which they give. We do not feel a sense of guilt. We do not feel that we must pay them back. Instead, we feel loved and freely given to.

People who want to care for others in physical need are usually "full of compassion." This is certainly true of those who have cared for us. Through-out the Gospels we see this quality in Jesus. He was described that way when he fed the hungry crowd in Matthew 14. As noted in the last study in this guide, the crowd was not starving to death. It was not in crisis. Jesus simply met a basic physical need. He was caring for them. He was "full of compassion."

The dictionary definition of compassion is, "to sorrow for the sufferings or troubles of another or others, with the urge to help; deep sympathy." Others have defined it as "using words and actions to make another person feel better." Compassion involves sensitivity to another's needs. It results in actions which will aid or help the individual.

Compassion differs from pity in that compassion is motivated by a positive genuine desire to comfort someone. A compassionate person takes action to do just that. Pity involves a contempt or a "looking down" on a person and rarely results in action.

Learning to care for others through action is what this study guide is about. The first part of this two-part guide is "Understanding Physical Needs." The principles in these studies establish a foundation for caring for others in physical need.

The first principle is that God cares for our physical needs; therefore physical needs are important. When we show care for others in need, we are showing God's care. We are doing what he wants us to do. The second principle is that we are whole people: body, soul and spirit. Physical needs affect not only my body, but my spirit and my emotions. The third principle is that the major reason for suffering and being in need is the fact that we live in a fallen and broken world. The fourth is that prayer is a vital resource when meeting needs.

Part two, "Meeting Physical Needs," also has four studies. We will look at Jesus healing a paralytic, Naaman being healed from leprosy, David's care for Jonathan's son Mephibosheth, and Jesus feeding the hungry crowd. In these case studies we will observe different ways people showed care to others. We will see the responses to that care. Based on what we learn in these passages, we will have opportunities to think about ways to care. And we will ask God to help us to care, in a sensitive way, for others in physical need.

This Bible study guide is for people who want to grow in their ability to care for those in physical need. It is also for those who sense a need to become compassionate people. May it be so for you.

Part 1/Understanding Physical Needs

1/God Cares for Physical Needs
Matthew 6:25-34

I remember the morning that our son Stephen tearfully announced that we did not have anything that his friends had. We did not have a VCR, video games or a dog. Lacking these kinds of things creates a sense of deprivation in our culture.

In our affluent society, what used to be considered luxuries are now in the category of needs. If we do not have the income to maintain two cars, a big house, dining out several times a week, and two televisions, we are in *need*. If the clothes on our backs even suggest a likeness to last year's wardrobe, we are in *need*. As these things become ingrained in our consciousness as needs, material gain becomes our goal in life and that is what we seek after.

The antidote? We must look into the Scriptures and see *need* from God's perspective. As we look, we will also see that he cares very much about our physical needs.

(By the way, we got the VCR. If we had gotten the dog, Andy and I would have felt great deprivation!)

---

1. How are you affected by society's definition of need?

2. Read Matthew 6:25-34. What are the specific physical needs mentioned in this passage?

3. What all does Jesus say about these needs (vv. 25-32)?

4. How would you define *need?*

5. What are your basic physical needs?

6. When have you been anxious about whether or not these needs would be met?

7. Do you have the ability to satisfy these needs for yourself? Why or why not?

8. Four times in these verses, Jesus says, "Do not worry." Why?

9. What do you think it means to seek God's kingdom and righteousness first?

10. How does knowing about God's care for your physical need equip you to help others who are in need?

11. Some of us are not only anxious about present need but worry about the future as well. In what ways might your worry about tomorrow be relieved as a result of what you have learned in this passage?

12. How can you help someone else not to worry about tomorrow?

Pray that God will make you sensitive to the person who is overly anxious about physical needs.

2/Caring for the Whole Person
Psalm 32

I lost weight—so much that I foolishly thought that I would never have to worry about overeating again. I couldn't sleep. I cried a lot. Yet there were times when I felt so dry inside that I couldn't cry. My emotional strength drained. I had nothing to give to others. I felt that God was completely out of reach. I had trouble praying. The Scriptures were like straw. In summary, my physical, emotional and spiritual energy were at an all-time low. I realized as never before that I am an integrated whole. I am body, soul and spirit.

When I am spiritually unsettled, my body and emotions are affected—as well as my spirit. When my emotions are out of kilter, my body and my relationship with God are out of kilter too. When I am physically ill, my emotional life and spirit also need extra attention.

1. When you are feeling low, what is your relationship with God like?

2. Read Psalm 32. As you look through the passage, what are all the phrases

that describe or relate to spiritual needs?

What about physical needs?

emotional needs?

3. How does David describe the happy person (vv. 1-2)?

4. What does it mean not to have deceit in one's spirit (v. 2)?

5. What was David like before he confessed his sins (vv. 3-4)?

6. What steps toward healing and forgiveness does the psalmist advocate and demonstrate (vv. 5-6)?

7. What problems can you predict if a person tried to achieve this kind of whole person healing, but refused to confess and turn from sin?

8. What were the physical and emotional as well as spiritual benefits of God's forgiveness to the psalmist (vv. 1-2, 5-10)?

9. What hope do verses 8-10 give for dealing with temptation in the future?

10. In the final verse of this passage David advocates rejoicing and singing. What effect does rejoicing and singing have on the whole person: body, emotion and spirit?

11. When have you experienced a lift in your whole being because of music that praised God?

12. As a result of studying this passage how can you more effectively care for those in physical need?

Ask God to help you discern the full range of needs in those whose lives you touch.

3/Praying for Healing
James 5:13-20

I have prayed fervently that someone would be healed, and I have seen God do just that. At other times, I have prayed for healing just as fervently—only to see that person continue to suffer and, eventually, to die. What makes the difference? Is it that God's glory is demonstrated differently in different situations? That his purpose and will is different in each case? Or simply that healing can only be complete when a believer reaches heaven through death?

I can't answer. But I do know that when I see people suffering all around me I long to help. I also know that God calls us to pray for one another, and not to pray is disobedience. In this passage, James gives us some practical help on how to pray for people in need.

1. In what kinds of situations are you most apt to pray?

2. Read James 5:13-20. What different uses of prayer do you see in these verses?

3. In verses 14-16, James discusses physical and spiritual healing. What are the steps to be taken in this process?

4. Why do you think it is important that the sick person initiate the healing process?

5. This passage suggests not only individual prayer and confession but praying with each other. What is the emotional, spiritual and physical value of confessing sin and praying together?

6. Would you call elders of your church for anointing, prayer and confession? Why or why not?

7. What do you think our attitude should be toward God as we pray for the sick?

8. How does Elijah illustrate the effectiveness of prayer?

9. Notice the different types of prayers that are mentioned in verses 13-20. How might each one of these be part of a healing process?

10. What seems to be the purpose of a community of believers who pray in this way?

11. What steps can you take to make praying for and with those in need more a part of your life?

12. Remember a time when you prayed for someone in need. What did you feel when you prayed?

What happened or didn't happen?

13. Do you find it easier to pray for spiritual, emotional or physical needs? Why?

Ask God for grace in this ministry, that he will make you faithful in prayer for and with others.

4/Why Suffering?
Genesis 3:1-21

I'd like to go back to the Garden of Eden and try it over again with a different script!" That is how my friend Linda expresses it. Wouldn't it be great to be able to give Adam and Eve another chance? What relief it could bring! The opportunity to play their parts just a bit differently would end all suffering. If only Adam and Eve had followed God's original script, suffering would have never come about in the first place.

But the fact is that we cannot go back. This is a scene that cannot be rerun. We are a fallen humanity, living in a fallen world, terribly broken by sin. And there is no clearer demonstration of this fallenness than the physical suffering that we see pressing in all around us.

1. What happens to you when you see someone physically in pain or disabled? (What do you feel? How do you react?)

2. Read Genesis 3:1-21. Compare what God said would happen if the man and woman ate from "the tree of the knowledge of good and evil" (Gen 2:9, 16-17) with what the serpent predicted would happen.

In what way did both predictions come true?

_____

3. What was wrong with the serpent's prediction and attitude toward God?

_____

4. Under Satan's influence, and using her own reason, Eve chose to eat the fruit that God told her not to eat. And Adam willingly stood by watching it happen, then ate some fruit himself. How is this similar to the way choices are made in our society today?

_____

5. Adam and Eve's relationship with God was broken because of their disobedience. The first result of their guilt was that they were embarrassed because they were naked before each other and before God. What does this indicate about the way sin changed their self-concepts?

6. How does self-concept affect physical well-being?

7. What other forms of human suffering result from the Fall?

8. What changes did God make in Adam and Eve's lifestyle as a result of their sin (vv. 14-21)?

9. What environmental changes, resulting from the Fall, continue to contribute to human suffering?

10. What do you think is the significance of God making "garments of skin" for Adam and Eve?

11. How can you make "garments of skin" for those in your life who are suffering physically?

12. How does an increased understanding of the effects of the Fall help you to handle your own suffering as well as that of others?

Ask God to help you view physical suffering in light of the Fall. Pray that he will strengthen you as you make "garments of skin" for people who are physically disabled or in pain.

Part 2/Meeting Physical Needs

5/The Paralytic

Mark 2:1-12

Timothy was six years old and sick with leukemia. One night, he took a turn for the worse and needed to be hospitalized. But a terrible ice storm had hit the city. Timothy's mother, a single parent, could not get her car started. So she called her pastor for help. He could not get his car started either. So the pastor called another man from the church, who not only started his car, but in those hazardous weather conditions, made his way to Timothy's house to take them to the hospital.

The roads were sheets of ice. They slid off the road, had two minor accidents, but they finally reached medical care.

In a relaxed moment after the trip, this sturdy Christian man appreciated the mother's words of gratitude. But it was Timothy's words that touched his spirit. Timothy asked, "Sir, are you Jesus?"

---

1. When have you been in physical need and have been cared for by someone else?

---

2. Read Mark 2:1-12. What evidence is there that the friends really cared about the paralytic (vv. 3-4)?

3. Think of someone in your life who is in physical need. What are obstacles that you must overcome to help take care of that person?

What do you learn from these four friends that might help you give care in that situation?

4. Of what value to the paralytic was the faith of his friends?

5. Sometimes we need to hang on to someone else's faith. When have you needed another person to believe God for you?

6. What actions and attitudes might you need if you are trying to believe God for someone else?

7. Though we assume that the four friends brought the paralytic to Jesus because of his physical need, what need did Jesus see as more critical (vv. 5, 9)?

Why do you think that the forgiveness of sin was a priority to Jesus?

8. How did Christ's approach to his needs suggest that the paralytic's body was connected to what is going on in his relationship with God (v. 5)?

9. The teachers of the Law questioned Jesus' authority to forgive sin and accused him of blasphemy when he did it. How did Jesus demonstrate his authority to forgive sins?

10. Why is it important to be "amazed" ourselves because of Christ's authority over both sin and physical illness?

11. What risk do we take when we bring a friend to Jesus?

12. As you think about caring for your friends in need by bringing them to Jesus, what difference does it make to you that Christ's perception of need, as well as his ability to meet those needs, is so great?

Ask God to help you to be amazed by who he is and what he does.

6/Naaman, the Leper
2 Kings 5:1-15

I knew Diana was growing when she was able to say, "I have come to realize that there are others all around me who are in pain. I am not the only one who is suffering. Until now I could not see the pain of others because I was so focused on mine." Often, the first step of being used by God in meeting others' needs is being able to identify those needs.

Three thousand years ago, Naaman, the pagan commander of a large army, was sick. In that setting, a take-charge man learned about need—from a servant girl. And he met a God who cared.

1. When you are in physical need what kinds of responses or activities from people communicate to you that someone cares?

2. Read 2 Kings 5:1-15. Describe Naaman and the servant girl.

3. As we consider perceiving and meeting needs, what is the significance of the vast difference in the social status of Naaman and that of the servant girl?

4. How do you respond to the possibility of being used by God to meet the needs of people in social, professional or economic groups different from your own?

5. What are ways that people reached out to Naaman throughout this passage?

6. Why was Naaman angry at Elisha (vv. 10-13)?

7. When have you been upset because of the way God chose to work when you or someone else was in need?

8. It was a servant who encouraged Naaman to do what the prophet had told him to do, though such action seemed to Naaman to be menial and "beneath" him. What right and simple things might people need encouragement to do, in order to get well?

9. What was Naaman's response when he was cured (v. 15)?

10. When you see God bring healing to your life, or to the life of someone else, how does your response compare to Naaman's?

11. In what ways can you give to God, as you desire to express your gratitude to him?

12. We have considered the benefits to Naaman of the help people gave him. What benefits do you think came to those who helped?

13. What benefits do you receive from seeing others helped?

Pray that God will make you sensitive to the needs of others and will help you to gently lead them in the right steps toward healing.

7/Mephibosheth
2 Samuel 9:1-13

We have very special friends coming to live with us this summer. We are excited about the time we will have with them. We are also anticipating a great time with their three sons, though we have never met them. But because we love Jackie and Steve, we also love Jeremy, Chris and Justin, and have already made a decision to embrace them as our own children. Because of our love for and loyalty to their parents, the boys already have a place in our care.

So it was with David and Mephibosheth. It was because of David's deep love for Jonathan that he gave special care to his son Mephibosheth.

---

1. When have you cared for someone that you did not know well? Why?

---

2. Consider David and Jonathan's relationship by glancing through 1 Samuel 18:1-4; 19:1-7 and 20:1-4. How would you describe their love and loyalty to each other?

3. Read 2 Samuel 9:1-13. In verses 1-6, what did David have to do to find Mephibosheth?

_____

4. How did David show kindness toward him (vv. 7-10)?

_____

5. How would you define kindness?

_____

6. Describe a time when someone was kind to you.

_____

7. Think of someone you know who is in physical need. What might you need to do to show kindness to that person?

_____

8. Why should your love for and loyalty to God motivate you to show kindness to that person?

9. How was Mephibosheth affected by David's kindness?

_____

10. What results would you like to see in a person to whom you show kindness?

_____

11. What risks did David take when he showed kindness to Mephibosheth?

_____

12. What kinds of risks do you take when you care for people that you do not know well?

_____

Pray for a person to whom you could show kindness. Ask God to work in that person's life as a result of your kindness.

8/A Hungry Crowd
Matthew 14:13-21

Most of us know nothing of real hunger. In Western society, we rarely see malnutrition. But one does not have to be "starving to death" to need to be fed. The crowd that Jesus fed was not "starving," but Jesus still took the time and effort to feed them—to meet their physical needs. But hunger is just one type of need. People all around us need all kinds of help. They are pressed by routine physical needs that we can help meet.

The feeding of a crowd came at a time in Christ's life when he himself was in great need. He had just received word that his cousin John the Baptist was dead. At a time when Jesus would much rather be alone with his own grief, he continued to minister to the crowd.

1. Under what kinds of circumstances is it difficult for you to meet the physical needs of others?

When is it easier?

2. Read Matthew 14:13-21. Jesus had just received word that John had been killed (see 14:1-12). How did he respond?

3. Compare Christ's response to the crowd with that of his disciples (vv. 14-19).

4. What does it mean to have compassion on someone?

5. When have you experienced someone's compassion toward you?

What was it like?

6. When do you respond to needy crowds more like Jesus, and when do you respond more like his disciples? Explain.

7. Choose a person that you know who has a need. What "loaves and fishes" (resources) do you have that could meet those needs?

---

8. When Jesus multiplied the disciples' loaves and fishes, not only was the crowd satisfied, but even the disciples ended up with much more than when they began. How have you experienced God's blessing in your own life as a result of helping someone else?

---

9. When you helped someone in need, what were the effects of your help on that person?

---

10. How can helping to meet someone's physical needs help you to know Christ better?

How have you experienced this? Explain.

Jesus did not ask the disciples to try to meet every need of every person they encountered. But this time he did want them to reach out, meet the needs and experience him in a new way. Ask God to make you sensitive to his leading as to what needs you can be instrumental in meeting during this next week.

Leader's Notes

Leading a Bible discussion can be an enjoyable and rewarding experience. But it can also be intimidating—especially if you've never done it before. If this is how you feel, you're in good company.

When God asked Moses to lead the Israelites out of Egypt, he replied, "O Lord, please send someone else to do it!" (Ex 4:13). But God's response to all of his servants—including you—is essentially the same: "My grace is sufficient for you" (2 Cor 12:9).

There is another reason you should feel encouraged. Leading a Bible discussion is not difficult if you follow certain guidelines. You don't need to be an expert on the Bible or a trained teacher. The suggestions listed below should enable you to effectively and enjoyably fulfill your role as leader.

Using Caring People Bible Studies
Where should you begin? A good starting place is *Handbook for Caring People*. This short book helps develop some basic caring skills like listening to and communicating to people who are in pain. Additionally, it will help you understand the stages that people in grief go through and how to help people who are suffering. Most of all, this book shows how to rely on God for the strength you need to care for others. At the end of each chapter, you'll find questions for individual or group use.

For the next step you might choose *Resources for Caring People* or *The*

Character of Caring People. Resources for Caring People will show how God empowers us to serve others through Scripture, prayer, the Holy Spirit and many other gifts. *The Character of Caring People* shows what the heart of the Christian caregiver is like. The concerns which emerge within the group during the studies will provide you with guidance for what to do next. All of the guides give help and encouragement to those who want to care for others, but different groups may find some guides more useful than others.

You might want to focus on specific concerns like *Caring for People in Grief* or *Caring for People in Conflict*. Or your group might choose to study topics which reflect areas they need to grow in. For instance, those who have sick friends or relatives or who simply want to be more sensitive to the physical needs that are all around us will find *Caring for Physical Needs* helpful. Others may want to know more about the spiritual concerns people have. *Caring for Spiritual Needs* is a great resource for this. For a biblical perspective on how God wants us to deal with emotional problems, you might choose *Caring for Emotional Needs*. The key is to remember that we all have these needs. Our physical condition affects us spiritually and emotionally. A spiritual problem can have physical and emotional consequences. By covering several of these guides in sequence, members of your group will develop a complete picture of what it means to be a caring Christian.

Preparing for the Study

1. Ask God to help you understand and apply the passage in your own life. Unless this happens, you will not be prepared to lead others. Pray too for the various members of the group. Ask God to open your hearts to the message of his Word and to motivate you to action.

2. Read the introduction to the entire guide to get an overview of the subject at hand and the issues which will be explored.

3. As you begin each study, read and reread the assigned Bible passage to familiarize yourself with it.

4. This study guide is based on the New International Version of the Bible. It will help you and the group if you use this translation as the basis for your study and discussion.

5. Carefully work through each question in the study. Spend time in meditation and reflection as you consider how to respond.

6. Write your thoughts and responses in the space provided in the study guide. This will help you to express your understanding of the passage clearly.

7. It might help you to have a Bible dictionary handy. Use it to look up any unfamiliar words, names or places. (For additional help on how to study a passage, see chapter five of *Leading Bible Discussions*, IVP.)

8. Take the response portion of each study seriously. Consider what this means for your life—what changes you might need to make in your lifestyle and/or actions you need to take in the world. Remember that the group will follow your lead in responding to the studies.

Leading the Study

1. Begin the study on time. Open with prayer, asking God to help the group to understand and apply the passage.

2. Be sure that everyone in your group has a study guide. Encourage the group to prepare beforehand for each discussion by reading the introduction to the guide and by working through the questions in the study.

3. At the beginning of your first time together, explain that these studies are meant to be discussions, not lectures. Encourage the members of the group to participate. However, do not put pressure on those who may be hesitant to speak during the first few sessions.

4. Have a group member read the introductory paragraph at the beginning of the discussion. This will orient the group to the topic of the study.

5. Every study begins with an "approach" question, which is meant to be asked before the passage is read. These questions are important for several reasons.

First, there is always a stiffness that needs to be overcome before people will begin to talk openly. A good question will break the ice.

Second, most people will have lots of different things going on in their minds (dinner, an important meeting coming up, how to get the car fixed) that will have nothing to do with the study. A creative question will get their attention and draw them into the discussion.

Third, approach questions can reveal where our thoughts or feelings need to be transformed by Scripture. That is why it is especially important not to read the passage before the approach question is asked. The passage will tend to color the honest reactions people would otherwise give because they are, of course, supposed to think the way the Bible does.

6. Have a group member read aloud the passage to be studied.

7. As you ask the questions, keep in mind that they are designed to be used just as they are written. You may simply read them aloud. Or you may prefer to express them in your own words. There may be times when it is appropriate to deviate from the study guide. For example, a question may have already been answered. If so, move on to the next question. Or someone may raise an important question not covered in the guide. Take time to discuss it, but try to keep the group from going off on tangents.

8. Avoid answering your own questions. If necessary, repeat or rephrase them until they are clearly understood. An eager group quickly becomes passive and silent if they think the leader will do most of the talking.

9. Don't be afraid of silence. People may need time to think about the question before formulating their answers.

10. Don't be content with just one answer. Ask, "What do the rest of you think?" or "anything else?" until several people have given answers to the question.

11. Acknowledge all contributions. Try to be affirming whenever possible. Never reject an answer. If it is clearly off-base, ask, "Which verse led you to that conclusion?" or again, "What do the rest of you think?"

12. Don't expect every answer to be addressed to you, even though this will probably happen at first. As group members become more at ease, they will begin to truly interact with each other. This is one sign of healthy discussion.

13. Don't be afraid of controversy. It can be very stimulating. If you don't resolve an issue completely, don't be frustrated. Move on and keep it in mind for later. A subsequent study may solve the problem.

14. Periodically summarize what the group has said about the passage. This helps to draw together the various ideas mentioned and gives continuity to the study. But don't preach.

15. Don't skip over the response questions. It's important that we not lose the focus of helping others even as we reflect on ourselves. Be willing to get things started by describing how you have been affected by the study.

16. Conclude your time together with conversational prayer. Ask for God's help in following through on the commitments you've made.

17. End on time. Many more suggestions and helps are found in *Small Group Leader's Handbook* and *Good Things Come in Small Groups* (both from IVP). Reading through one of these books would be worth your time.

Listening to Emotional Pain

Caring People Bible Studies are designed to take seriously the pain and struggle that is part of life. People will experience a variety of emotions during these studies. Keep in mind that you are not expected to act as a professional counselor. However, part of your role as group leader may be to listen to emotional pain. Listening is a gift which you can give to a person who is hurting. For many people, it is not an easy gift to give. The following suggestions will help you to listen more effectively to people in emotional pain.

1. Remember that you are not responsible to take the pain away. People in helping relationships often feel that they are being asked to make the other person feel better. This may be related to the helper not being comfortable with painful feelings.

2. Not only are you not responsible to take the pain away, one of the things people need most is an opportunity to face and to experience the pain in their lives. Many have spent years denying their pain and running from it. Healing can come when we are able to face our pain in the presence of someone who cares about us. Rather than trying to take the pain away, then, commit yourself to listening attentively as it is expressed.

3. Realize that some group members may not feel comfortable with others' expressions of sadness or anger. You may want to acknowledge that such emotions are uncomfortable, but say that learning to feel our own pain is often the first step in helping others with their pain.

4. Be very cautious about giving answers and advice. Advice and answers may make you feel better or feel competent, but they may also minimize people's problems and their painful feelings. Simple solutions rarely work, and they can easily communicate "You should be better now" or "You shouldn't really be talking about this."

5. Be sure to communicate direct affirmation any time people talk about their painful emotions. It takes courage to talk about our pain because it creates anxiety for us. It is a great gift to be trusted by those who are struggling.

The following notes refer to specific questions in the study:

Study 1. God Cares for Physical Needs. Matthew 6:25-34.

Purpose: To see how God meets physical needs and speaks to our anxiety about them.

Question 3. He says a lot. Scan all of verses 25-32.

Question 4. According to Webster, "necessity, lack of something required, a condition requiring relief or supply, an urgent requirement of something essential that is lacking." Help the group differentiate between need and desire or even luxury.

Question 6. Webster points out that worry is derived from the English phrase, "to gnaw like a wolf at the throat of its victim." Anxiety and worry are common enemies in today's society.

Question 9. The kingdom of God is the rule of King Jesus in our hearts and on earth as in heaven. It is living by his values, as he would live.

Question 12. Helping someone not to worry may involve more than words. It may involve action as well: a carload of groceries, a check, a job lead, a social service referral. Be sure that your group discusses both words *and* actions.

Study 2. Caring for the Whole Person. Psalm 32.

Purpose: To see that each person is a physically, emotionally and spiritually integrated being. To understand that all parts of our being are affected when one part is hurting.

Question 2. This question is intended to be an overview of the passage, so do not linger too long on it. The purpose of the question is to see David's physical, emotional and spiritual condition, and how his emotions and body are affected by a broken relationship with God. The psalm also makes clear that David's whole being was changed when this relationship was healed. You will discuss details more thoroughly as you progress through the study.

Question 5. Help the group to bring out the emotional and physical aspects as well as the spiritual results of David's unconfessed sin.

Question 8. God does not leave us alone to deal with sin and temptation by ourselves. He promises us guidance, instruction and protection.

Study 3. Praying for Healing. James 5:13-20.

Purpose: To grow in praying for others in physical need.

General Note: Though this study only covers eight verses, you will need to watch your time carefully. Several potentially controversial topics will come up—among them, faith-healing and the church's role in healing. Yet the place of prayer in our lives and how we pray for others deserves adequate time. Keep one eye on the clock and the other on your group. This is a pastoral section of James, so set a pastoral tone.

Question 2. Use this question to survey the passage. Your group should find some reference to prayer in almost every verse. Don't forget to notice prayers of both grief and praise in verse 13.

Question 3. Note on anointing with oil: Olive oil was used both internally and externally as a medicine. It was also used in religious ceremonies of consecration (Ex 29:2) and purification (Lev 14:10-18). It symbolized gladness, comfort and spiritual nourishment.

Question 4. It is important to note that the sick person initiates the healing process for several reasons: (1) people are psychologically most ready to receive help if they see their own need, (2) helpers should be cautious about forcing help on those who do not want it, (3) James makes it clear that this is one permissible way to deal with illness (there is no *must* in the sentence). These points should flow from the questions here as the discussion progresses.

Question 8. If your group is unfamiliar with Elijah, refer to 1 Kings 17:1; 18:1, 42-45.

Question 10. Several purposes appear in the passage. Among them: mutual help (v. 13), mutual praise (v. 13), healing (v. 15), forgiveness (v. 15). But perhaps the most important purpose appears in verses 19-20. Here we see a mutual moral accountability and therefore a vast protection against wandering from the faith.

Study 4. Why Suffering? Genesis 3:1-21.

Purpose: To understand that though there are many effects of suffering, both good and bad, there is one basic cause: we are fallen people, living in a fallen world.

Question 3. The problem with the serpent's prediction was his deceitfulness. He told only part of the truth in order to influence Eve in the wrong direction.

Satan's attitude toward God was full of arrogance, rebellion, disobedience, and questions about God's authority.

Question 7. Many forms of physical suffering result from the Fall. Allow the group time to discuss as many of these as possible. You should think of such things as aging and death, deterioration of our minds and body, and broken relationships that cause stress. These in turn bring on such symptoms as high blood pressure, heart attacks and ulcers. Other more direct results of disobedience to God's commands include: venereal disease, murder, robbery and other violence.

Question 9. In question 7, you discussed human suffering that resulted from the Fall. In this question, broaden the discussion to also include environmental changes.

Study 5. The Paralytic. Mark 2:1-12.

Purpose: To see how friends cared for the physical needs of the paralytic, and to learn how we can care for people in physical need in the same ways.

Question 5. Not everyone in the group will have had the experience of needing someone else to believe God for them. But even one or two stories of this nature will encourage this kind of giving as well as instruct others in how it might be done.

Question 6. This kind of ministry involves praying faithfully for and with that person (if he or she is *open to* that). It might involve gentle words of hope that the day will come again when God will reveal himself and the person will be able to believe for himself. It might mean sharing from Scripture about God, when this is appropriate, or encouraging the person to look into Scripture with you. It means maintaining a spirit and attitude of hope when that person feels hopeless. It means avoiding a Pollyanna attitude of "Don't worry; everything will be all right."

Question 7. The second part of this question allows for speculation; the answer is not clear in this passage. The paralytic's relationship to God was obviously important to Jesus and apparently to the paralytic. There is always the possibility that the four men and/or the paralytic were well aware of his need to have his sins forgiven. Dealing with the sin issue certainly raised the issue of Christ's authority as God. The teachers of the Law were quick to notice.

Question 8. This question is included to further illustrate the truth from study 2, "Caring for the Whole Person." It should not take a lot of discussion time.

Question 10. If I am not experiencing the reality of the amazement of Jesus' power, how can I effectively bring others to him?

Question 12. I can bring my friends to Jesus with great confidence. Jesus will meet the more obvious needs, but also those not so overt. Yet of even greater importance, Jesus will see and respond to the needs that I am not aware of in my friend.

This knowledge should make me desire and seek Christ's wisdom, discernment and insight as I try to meet the needs of people.

Study 6. Naaman, the Leper. 2 Kings 5:1-15.

Purpose: To observe from this story how people perceived Naaman's need and then encouraged him through each step that he should take to be cured by God.

Questions 3-4. We are often blind to the needs of leaders or of those we consider to be "above us" in any way. We might eliminate the possibility of being used by God to minister to such people when God could desire to use us.

Question 6. "Ritual washings were practiced among Eastern religions as a purification rite. . . . Naaman was to wash in the muddy waters of the Jordan River, demonstrating that there was no natural connection between the washing and the desired healing. Perhaps it also suggested that one needed to pass through the Jordan, as Israel had done (Jos 3—4), in order to obtain healing from the God of Israel." However, Naaman expected to be healed by Elisha's magical powers, rather than by the power of God (Kenneth Barker, gen. ed., *The NIV Study Bible* [Grand Rapids: Zondervan, 1985], pp. 531-32).

Question 8. This encouragement could be in the area of things as simple as getting adequate rest, eating right, eliminating pressures, getting schedules and commitments under control, healing broken relationships, or getting themselves some professional help.

Question 10. Be sure that your group considers all forms of healing—not just physical well-being.

Gratitude to God and to others is often missing in today's society. We are hardly aware of his great giving to us. It is true humility to acknowledge who God is, his great work in us, and to express gratitude to him.

Study 7. Mephibosheth. 2 Samuel 9:1-13.
Purpose: To seek to show kindness to people in need because of our love and loyalty to God.

Question 2. Allow a few minutes to glance through the passage. Then discuss David and Jonathan's relationship. This will set the tone for the study in an important way. It is David's relationship with Jonathan that was the basis for David's showing kindness to Mephibosheth. It is also a model of how our love for God and our loyalty to him should affect our care for people in need.

Question 3. The point of this question is that it was not a simple thing to even find Mephibosheth. It took effort. Lo Debar was a great distance from where David was living.

Question 4. David's action was not just a token gesture, but was extravagant—again, symbolic of his love for Jonathan.

Question 5. According to the dictionary, *kindness* is the state or habit of being sympathetic, friendly, gentle, tenderhearted, generous, cordial. Kindness is not action imposed on another person. It springs from a sensitivity to another person's view of his own needs—and a willingness to meet those needs.

Question 6. Sharing an experience of someone being kind to them will remind the group members of what it is to receive kindness. (Be prepared for both positive and negative reactions.) This will set the stage for discussing the importance of being sensitively kind to someone else.

Question 8. At the very core of our showing kindness to others is our love for and loyalty to God. Even as David's deep love for Jonathan motivated him to be kind to Mephibosheth, so our deep love and loyalty to God is our motivation for being kind to his people.

Question 9. Part of the answer is based on what is said (vv. 7-12). There is also room for the group to speculate on how they think David's kindness would affect him.

Question 10. Having a vision for those we are involved with can be helpful and motivating. It can give direction on what kind of help is needed. It is satisfying to see good results. It must not, however, create a sense of obligation on the part of the one being helped.

Question 11. David took several risks in showing kindness to Mephibosheth. Because he was a descendant of Saul's, Mephibosheth could have been a contender for the throne. And not only did David bring Mephibosheth into his household, he also accepted Ziba and his fifteen sons and twenty servants. And Ziba had been loyal to Saul.

If members of your group express interest in whether these risks eventually caught up with David, you can suggest that they read the outcome of the story at a later time. See 2 Samuel 16:1-4 and 19:17-30.

Study 8. A Hungry Crowd. Matthew 14:13-21.
Purpose: To appreciate Christ's feeding a crowd of people—even though the people were not starving. To integrate into our lives ways of meeting the routine physical needs of those around us.

Question 3. Look for both similarities and differences.

Question 4. The dictionary definition of *compassion* is, "to sorrow for the sufferings or trouble of another or others, with the urge to help; deep sympathy." Another definition is, "using words and actions to make another person feel better." Compassion is motivated by a positive desire to comfort through action. It differs from pity in that pity usually looks down on someone and rarely results in action.

Question 5. Sharing from personal experience about compassion can have many results that will help in this discussion. Depending on how much compassion has been extended to them, it might help people in the group to realize how rare compassion is. It can demonstrate how needed and helpful compassion is as people share about times that they have experienced it from others. It can give practical ideas on how to show compassion to others.

Question 7. Use this question to help the group realize that physical needs go beyond illness and hunger. People need help when they are feeling overwhelmed by life. We can help by taking care of their children to give them time to themselves—or to give mom and dad time with each other. Other examples include: taking in meals when a person is tired or sick, helping with housework, yardwork or remodeling. These are all ways that can help someone feel better. Sometimes showing compassion or meeting physical needs involves stepping in and taking over rather than just saying, "Let me know what I can do."

About the Author

Phyllis J. Le Peau is a registered nurse and a former Nurses Christian Fellowship staffworker. Currently, she is assistant program director for Wellness, Inc. Phyllis is also the author of the Fruit of the Spirit Bible Studies Kindness, Gentleness and Joy (Zondervan) and coauthor of Disciplemakers' Handbook (IVP). With her husband, Andy, she has coauthored One Plus One Equals One and the LifeGuide® Bible Studies Ephesians and James (IVP/SU). She and her husband live in Downers Grove, Illinois, with their four children.

Caring People Bible Studies from InterVarsity Press
By Phyllis J. Le Peau

Handbook for Caring People (coauthored by Bonnie J. Miller). This book provides simple, time-tested principles for dealing with the pain, the questions and the crises people face. You will get the basic tools for communication plus some practical suggestions. Questions for group discussion are at the end of each chapter.

Resources for Caring People. Through God, we have the resources we need to help others. God has given us Scripture, prayer, the Holy Spirit, listening and acceptance. This guide will show you how he works through people like you every day. 8 studies.

The Character of Caring People. The key to caring is character. These Bible studies will show you how to focus on the gifts of caring which God has given you—such as hospitality, generosity and encouragement. 8 studies.

Caring for Spiritual Needs. A relationship with God. Meaning and purpose. Belonging. Love. Assurance. These are just some of the spiritual needs that we all have. This Bible study guide will help you learn how these needs can be met in your life and in the lives of others. 9 studies.

Caring for Emotional Needs. We think we have to act like we have it all together, yet sometimes we are lonely, afraid or depressed. Christians have emotional needs just like everyone else. This Bible study guide shows how to find emotional health for ourselves and how to help others. 9 studies.

Caring for Physical Needs. When we are sick or when our basic needs for food, clothing and adequate housing are not being met, our whole being—body, spirit and emotion—is affected. When we care for the physical needs of others, we are showing God's love. These Bible studies will help you learn to do that. 8 studies.

Caring for People in Conflict. Divided churches. Broken friendships. Angry children. Torn marriages. We all have to deal with conflict and the emotions which accompany it. These studies will show you how God can bring healing and reconciliation. 9 studies.

Caring for People in Grief. Because sin brought death into the world, we all have to look into death's ugly face at one time or another. These Bible studies cover the issues which consume those who are grieving—fear, peace, grace and hope—and show you how to provide them with comfort. 9 studies.